# CSET
## 140

# Art Sample Subtest
## Teacher Certification Exam

**By:** Sharon Wynne, M.S
Southern Connecticut State University

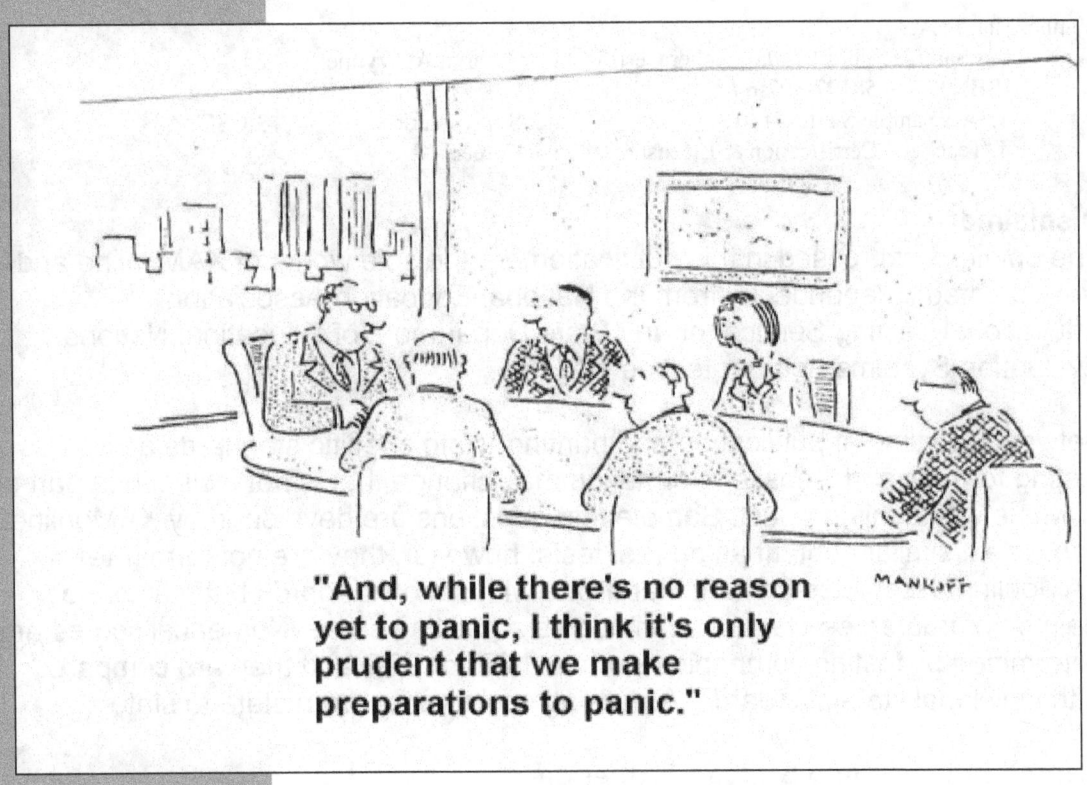

"And, while there's no reason yet to panic, I think it's only prudent that we make preparations to panic."

# XAMonline, INC.
Boston

To obtain permission(s) to use the material from this work for any purpose including workshops or seminars, please submit a written request to:

XAMonline, Inc.
21 Orient Ave.
Melrose, MA 02176
Toll Free 1-800-509-4128
Email: info@xamonline.com
Web www.xamonline.com
Fax: 1-781-662-9268

Library of Congress Cataloging-in-Publication Data

Wynne, Sharon A.
    Art Sample Subtest 140: Teacher Certification / Sharon A. Wynne. -2nd ed.
    ISBN 978-1-58197-397-6
    1. Art Sample Subtest 140.          2. Study Guides.          3.CSET
    4. Teachers' Certification & Licensure.     5. Careers

**Disclaimer:**
The opinions expressed in this publication are the sole works of XAMonline and were created independently from the National Education Association, Educational Testing Service, or any State Department of Education, National Evaluation Systems or other testing affiliates.

Between the time of publication and printing, state specific standards as well as testing formats and website information may change that is not included in part or in whole within this product. Sample test questions are developed by XAMonline and reflect similar content as on real tests; however, they are not former tests. XAMonline assembles content that aligns with state standards but makes no claims nor guarantees teacher candidates a passing score. Numerical scores are determined by testing companies such as NES or ETS and then are compared with individual state standards. A passing score varies from state to state.

**Printed in the United States of America**

CSET: Art Sample Subtest 140
ISBN: 978-1-58197-397-6

## *About the Subject Assessments*

## CSET™: Subject Assessment in the Art examination

**Purpose:** The assessments are designed to test the knowledge and competencies of prospective secondary level teachers. The question bank from which the assessment is drawn is undergoing constant revision. As a result, your test may include questions that will not count towards your score.

**Test Version:** There are three versions of subject assessment for Art tests in California. Art Subtest I (140) emphasizes comprehension in Artistic Perception; Historical and Cultural Context of the Visual Arts; Aesthetic Valuing. Art Subtest II (141) emphasizes comprehension in Creative Expression; Connections Relationships and Applications; History and Theories of Learning in Art. Both exams taken together represent the Single Subject Teaching Credential authorizing the teaching of Art coursework. The Art examination guide is based on a typical knowledge level of persons who have completed a *bachelor's degree program* in Art.

**Time Allowance and Format:** You will have 5 hours to finish the test. Part of the test will consist of multiple-choice questions; part of the test will consist of focused and extended constructed-response questions. There are 50 multiple-choice questions, 3 focused constructed-response questions and 1 extended constructed-response question

**Weighting:** There are 20 multiple-choice questions and 1 extended constructed-response questions in Subtest I for Aesthetic Valuing; 15 multiple-choice questions and 1 focused constructed-response questions in Historical and Cultural Context of the Visual Arts; 15 multiple-choice questions and 2 focused constructed-response questions (1 is a drawing) for Artistic Perception.

**Additional Information about the CSET Assessments:** The CSET™ series subject assessments are developed *National Evaluation Systems.* They provide additional information on the CSET series assessments, including registration, preparation and testing procedures, study materials such topical guides that have about 34 pages of information including approximately 19 additional sample questions.

## TABLE OF CONTENTS

## Great Study and Testing Tips!

*What* to study in order to prepare for the subject assessments is the focus of this study guide but equally important is *how* you study.

You can increase your chances of truly mastering the information by taking some simple, but effective steps.

## Study Tips:

**1. <u>Some foods aid the learning process</u>.** Foods such as milk, nuts, seeds, rice, and oats help your study efforts by releasing natural memory enhancers called CCKs (*cholecystokinin*) composed of *tryptophan*, *choline*, and *phenylalanine*. All of these chemicals enhance the neurotransmitters associated with memory. Before studying, try a light, protein-rich meal of eggs, turkey, and fish. All of these foods release the memory enhancing chemicals. The better the connections, the more you comprehend.

Likewise, before you take a test, stick to a light snack of energy boosting and relaxing foods. A glass of milk, a piece of fruit, or some peanuts all release various memory-boosting chemicals and help you to relax and focus on the subject at hand.

**2. <u>Learn to take great notes</u>.** A by-product of our modern culture is that we have grown accustomed to getting our information in short doses (i.e. TV news sound bites or USA Today style newspaper articles.)

Consequently, we've subconsciously trained ourselves to assimilate information better in <u>neat little packages</u>. If your notes are scrawled all over the paper, it fragments the flow of the information. Strive for clarity. Newspapers use a standard format to achieve clarity. Your notes can be much clearer through use of proper formatting. A very effective format is called the *"Cornell Method."*

> Take a sheet of loose-leaf lined notebook paper and draw a line all the way down the paper about 1-2" from the left-hand edge.

> Draw another line across the width of the paper about 1-2" up from the bottom. Repeat this process on the reverse side of the page.

Look at the highly effective result. You have ample room for notes, a left hand margin for special emphasis items or inserting supplementary data from the textbook, a large area at the bottom for a brief summary, and a little rectangular space for just about anything you want.

3. <u>**Get the concept then the details.**</u> Too often we focus on the details and don't gather an understanding of the concept. However, if you simply memorize only dates, places, or names, you may well miss the whole point of the subject.

A key way to understand things is to put them in your own words. If you are working from a textbook, automatically summarize each paragraph in your mind. If you are outlining text, don't simply copy the author's words.

*Rephrase* them in your own words. You remember your own thoughts and words much better than someone else's, and subconsciously tend to associate the important details to the core concepts.

4. <u>**Ask Why?**</u> Pull apart written material paragraph by paragraph and don't forget the captions under the illustrations.

Example: If the heading is "Stream Erosion", flip it around to read "Why do streams erode?" Then answer the questions.

If you train your mind to think in a series of questions and answers, not only will you learn more, but it also helps to lessen the test anxiety because you are used to answering questions.

5. <u>**Read for reinforcement and future needs**</u>. Even if you only have 10 minutes, put your notes or a book in your hand. Your mind is similar to a computer; you have to input data in order to have it processed. *By reading, you are creating the neural connections for future retrieval.* The more times you read something, the more you reinforce the learning of ideas.

Even if you don't fully understand something on the first pass, *your mind stores much of the material for later recall.*

6. <u>**Relax to learn so go into exile.**</u> Our bodies respond to an inner clock called biorhythms. Burning the midnight oil works well for some people, but not everyone.

If possible, set aside a particular place to study that is free of distractions. Shut off the television, cell phone, pager and exile your friends and family during your study period.

If you really are bothered by silence, try background music. Light classical music at a low volume has been shown to aid in concentration over other types. Music that evokes pleasant emotions without lyrics are highly suggested. Try just about anything by Mozart. It relaxes you.

**7. <u>Use arrows not highlighters</u>.** At best, it's difficult to read a page full of yellow, pink, blue, and green streaks. Try staring at a neon sign for a while and you'll soon see that the horde of colors obscure the message.

A quick note, a brief dash of color, an underline, and an arrow pointing to a particular passage is much clearer than a horde of highlighted words.

**8. <u>Budget your study time</u>.** Although you shouldn't ignore any of the material, *allocate your available study time in the same ratio that topics may appear on the test.*

## Testing Tips:

1. <u>**Get smart, play dumb**</u>. **Don't read anything into the question.** Don't make an assumption that the test writer is looking for something else than what is asked. Stick to the question as written and don't read extra things into it.

2. <u>**Read the question and all the choices *twice* before answering the question**</u>. You may miss something by not carefully reading, and then re-reading both the question and the answers.

If you really don't have a clue as to the right answer, leave it blank on the first time through. Go on to the other questions, as they may provide a clue as to how to answer the skipped questions.

If later on, you still can't answer the skipped ones . . . ***Guess.*** The only penalty for guessing is that you *might* get it wrong. Only one thing is certain; if you don't put anything down, you will get it wrong!

3. <u>**Turn the question into a statement**</u>. Look at the way the questions are worded. The syntax of the question usually provides a clue. Does it seem more familiar as a statement rather than as a question? Does it sound strange?

By turning a question into a statement, you may be able to spot if an answer sounds right, and it may also trigger memories of material you have read.

4. <u>**Look for hidden clues**</u>. It's actually very difficult to compose multiple-foil (choice) questions without giving away part of the answer in the options presented.

In most multiple-choice questions you can often readily eliminate one or two of the potential answers. This leaves you with only two real possibilities and automatically your odds go to Fifty-Fifty for very little work.

5. <u>**Trust your instincts**</u>. For every fact that you have read, you subconsciously retain something of that knowledge. On questions that you aren't really certain about, go with your basic instincts. **Your first impression on how to answer a question is usually correct.**

6. <u>**Mark your answers directly on the test booklet**</u>. Don't bother trying to fill in the optical scan sheet on the first pass through the test.

*Just be very careful not to miss-mark your answers when you eventually transcribe them to the scan sheet.*

7. <u>**Watch the clock**</u>! You have a set amount of time to answer the questions. Don't get bogged down trying to answer a single question at the expense of 10 questions you can more readily answer.

**THIS PAGE BLANK**

## Competency 1
Knowledge of the processes of drawing

**Skill 1.1**
Identify and demonstrate knowledge of materials, tools, processes and <u>drawing visual characteristics</u>.

**Question 1.1**
The term used to describe the many degrees of shading between black and white is

    A. intensity

    B. cloisonne

    C. chiaroscuro

    D. hue

**Rationale A**

**Skill 1.2**
Demonstrate an understanding of the organization of visual elements and the selection of media for <u>expressive drawing effect.</u>

**Question 1.2**
The amount of light reflected by a hue is known as

    A. veduta

    B. volute

    C. value

    D. tempera

**Rationale C**

**Skill 1.3**
Identify <u>drawing</u> techniques and methods appropriate for k-12 instruction.

**Question 1.3**
Everything in nature adheres to the cone, the cylinder, and the curve. That statement was said by the painter

      A. Monet

      B. Cezanne

      C. Chavdin

      D. Picasso

**Rationale  B**

**<u>Competency 2</u>**
Knowledge of the process of <u>painting</u>.

**Skill 2.1**
Identify and demonstrate knowledge of painting materials, tools, processes and visual characteristics.

**Question 2.1**
A NEWER painting medium is

      A. synthetic resin paints

      B. vegetable dyes

      C. casein paints

      D. gold leaf

**Rationale  A**

**Skill 2.2**
Demonstrate an understanding of the organization of <u>visual elements of painting</u> and the selection of media for <u>expressive effect.</u>

**Question 2.2**

Paintings with the emphasis on inner emotions, sensations, or ideas rather than actual appearances is called

      A. impressionism

      B. futurism

      C. expressionism

      D. extentialism

**Rationale  C**

**Skill 2.3**
Identify <u>painting techniques</u> and methods appropriate for k-12 instruction.

**Question 2.3**
Bright colors, sharp diagonal movements, constantly moving forms and melodramatic lighting BEST describe

      A. expressionist

      B. op

      C. genre

      D. French romantic

**Rationale  D**

## Competency 3
**Knowledge of the processes of sculpture.**

### Skill 3.1
Identify and demonstrate knowledge of <u>sculpture</u> materials, tools, <u>processes</u> and visual characteristics.

### Question 3.1
Assembling sheet brass sculptures is safest in a classroom situation when the teacher uses the method of

    A. brazing

    B. welding

    C. soldering

    D. embossing

**Rationale  C**

### Skill 3.2
Demonstrate an understanding of the organization of visual elements and the selection of media for expressive <u>sculpture</u> effects.

### Question 3.2
The LEAST important expectation of a lesson in modeling the human figure is

    A. developing the ability to express a human gesture in form

    B. achieving a proficiency in anatomical construction

    C. becoming more sensitive to form relationships in sculpture

    D. discovering more about the applications of the media

**Rationale  B**

**Skill 3.3**
**Identify <u>sculpture</u> techniques and methods appropriate for k-12 instruction.**

**Question 3.3**
**The MAIN concept to stress in a lesson on sculpture for beginners is**

      A. compact and unified form

      B. realistic detail

      C. imaginative treatment

      D. grooved forms

**Rationale  A**

<u>**Competency 4**</u>
**Knowledge of the processes of printmaking.**

**Skill 4.1**
**Identify and demonstrate knowledge of <u>printmaking</u> materials, tools, processes and visual characteristics.**

**Question 4.1**
**If the background of a dry point etching is too dark, the cause is probably**

      A. too much ink

      B. too much roller pressure

      C. inadequate wiping

      D. inadequate paper conditioning

**Rationale  C**

**Skill 4.2**
**Demonstrate an understanding of the organization of visual elements and the selection of media for expressive <u>printmaking</u> effect.**

**Question 4.2**
**In silk screen printing, tusche is used in making a _____**

      A. paper

      B. washout

      C. film

      D. photograph

**Rationale  B**

**Skill 4.3**
**Identify <u>printmaking</u> techniques and methods appropriate for k-12 instruction.**

**Question 4.3**
**Adjusting the impression of a print run can BEST be accomplished by**

      A. make-ready

      B. moving the grippers

      C. tightening the guides

      D. adjusting the platen

**Rationale  A**

## COMPETENCY 5
**Knowledge of the process of ceramics.**

**Skill 5.1**
Identify and demonstrate knowledge of <u>ceramic</u> materials, tools, processes used in ceramic production.

**Question 5.1**
The process used to make earthenware waterproof is known as

      A.  glazing

      B.  molding

      C.  firing

      D.  bisque

**Rationale  A**

**Skill 5.2**
Demonstrate an understanding of <u>ceramics</u> in the selection of media for expressive effect.

**Question 5.2**
Of the following, the oxide that is used to produce a glaze with red tones is

      A.  vanadium oxide

      B.  iron oxide

      C.  nickel oxide

      D.  cobalt oxide

**Rationale  B**

**Skill 5.3**
**Identify techniques and methods appropriate for k-12 <u>ceramic</u> instruction.**

**Question 5.3**
**Ceramic sculpture that is NOT to be fired is often supported with**

>   A.  star stilts

>   B.  bridging

>   C.  an armature

>   D.  a wire looped tool

**Rationale C**

**<u>Competency 6</u>**
**Knowledge of the processes using fiber.**

**Skill 6.1**
**Identify and demonstrate knowledge of materials, tools of <u>fiber</u> processes**

**Question 6.1**
**In weaving, a series of threads that lie in a vertical position is called the**

>   A.  weft

>   B.  warp

>   C.  bye-spokes

>   D.  shag

**Rationale B**

**Skill 6.2**
**Demonstrate an understanding of the organization of visual elements and the selection of media for expressive <u>fiber</u> effect.**

**Question 6.2**
**The character of fabrics used in stage costumes is important. All of these combinations are correct EXCEPT**

      A.  Chiffon – drapes well in fine folds

      B.  Buckram – gives deep, soft folds

      C.  Burlap – coarse and stiff, drapes reluctantly

      D.  Satin – catches light that accents folds

**Rationale B**

**Skill 6.3**
**Identify techniques and methods appropriate for k-12 <u>fiber</u> instruction.**

**Question 6.3**
**A term applied to pattern in weaving is**

      A.  applique

      B.  batik

      C.  jacquard

      D.  petit point

**Rationale C**

## Competency 7
Knowledge of the processes using <u>metals</u>.

## Skill 7.1
Identify and demonstrate knowledge of materials, tools, processes employed in metal fabrication and decoration.

## Question 7.1
Of the following materials used in early American crafts, the one that was NOT included was

      A. wrought iron

      B. hammered copper

      C. painted tin

      D. pewter

**Rationale D**

## Skill 7.2
Demonstrate an understanding of the organization of visual elements and the selection of media for expressive effect.

## Question 7.2
Copper and brass may be darkened by treatment with a solution of

      A. hydrochloric acid

      B. floor wax

      C. potassium sulphide

      D. hydrogen peroxide

**Rationale C**

**Skill 7.3**
Identify techniques and methods appropriate for k-12 <u>metals instruction.</u>

**Question 7.3**
All of the following terms are concerned with metal work EXCEPT

    A. champleve

    B. cloisonné

    C. repousse

    D. batik

**Rationale D**

<u>Competency 8</u>
Knowledge of the processes of mixed media.

**Skill 8.1**
Identify and demonstrate knowledge of materials, tools, techniques used in mixed media.

**Question 8.1**
Jewelry, potentially could be a mixed media project. The technique of ornamenting in which small grains of metal, usually gold, are soldered to a flat surface is:

    A. gouache

    B. granulation

    C. hatching

    D. iconostasis

**Rationale B**

**Skill 8.2**
**Demonstrate an understanding of the organization of visual elements and the selection of media for expressive effect.**

**Question 8.2**
**The internet brings so many new possibilities to the classroom. The term used to visualize a recreation of audio-video is:**

    A. nic card

    B. scanning from digital cameras

    C. streaming video

    D. live instant teleconferencing

**Rationale C**

**Skill 8.3**
**Identify techniques and methods appropriate for k-12 <u>mixed media</u> instruction.**

**Question 8.3**
**Software can be used for research as well as to obtain scanned material for incorporation into a work of art that is mixed media based. Common software used for graphic representations is:**

    A. Photo shop

    B. Excel

    C. Works

    D. Access

**Rationale A**

<u>Competency 9</u>
**Knowledge of the processes of <u>graphic design</u>**

**Skill 9.1**
**Identify and demonstrate knowledge of <u>graphic arts design </u>processes, tools and materials.**

**Question 9.1**
**In the graphic arts, the contrariety between grease and water makes possible the**

    A. dry point

    B. serigraph

    C. monotype

    D. lithograph

**Rationale D**

**Skill 9.2**
**Demonstrate an understanding of the organization of visual elements and the selection of media for expressive graphic arts effect.**

**Question 9.2**
**Mezzotint, aquatint and stipple are**

    A. names of engraving tools

    B. sheets of overlay used in advertising art

    C. techniques of modern photo- engraving

    D. processes designed to produce tonal effects

**Rationale D**

**Skill 9.3**
**Identify techniques and methods appropriate for k-12 graphic arts design instruction.**

**Question 9.3**
A method of reproducing drawings by which the incised lines are the parts which are printed is classified as _____ printing.

      A. intaglio

      B. relief

      C. paleographic

      D. offset

**Rationale A**

**Competency 10**
**Knowledge of the processes of architecture and environmental design.**

**Skill 10.1**
**Identify and demonstrate knowledge of materials and processes employed in architecture and in environmental design.**

**Question 10.1**
**Solar heated houses means houses**

      A. with excellent insulation

      B. that faces west

      C. with radiant heating

      D. oriented to make use of the sun's rays

**Rationale D**

**Skill 10.2**
**Demonstrate an understanding of the organization of visual elements of** <u>architecture</u> **an environmental design.**

**Question 10.2**
**Gothic architecture is closely associated with**

      A. column

      B. dome

      C. gargoyle

      D. open meeting areas

**Rationale C**

**Skill 10.3**
**Identify techniques and methods appropriate for k-12** <u>architecture instruction</u>.

**Question 10.3**
**A room too long for its width can be made to appear wider by using a _____ color on the _____.**

      A. warm; short walls

      B. bright; ceiling

      C. warm; walls

      D. bright; long walls

**Rationale A**

Competency 11
Knowledge of the processes of photography.

Skill 11.1
Identify and demonstrate knowledge of drawing materials, tools, processes of the photographic arts.

Question 11.1
What is one of the three basic liquids needed for processing a photograph?

      A. redeveloper

      B. Hypo silver solution

      C. Fixative basic bath

      D. sulfuric acid

Rationale  B

Skill 11.2
Demonstrate an understanding of the organization of visual elements and the selection of media for photographic expressive effect.

Question 11.2
If you take a picture on a sunny day your film results will show

      A. flat gray

      B. medium gray

      C. more contrast

      D. less contrast

Rationale  C

**Skill 11.3**
**Identify techniques and methods appropriate for k-12 photographic instruction.**

**Question 11.3**
**A good project for a beginning class in photography would be to make**

    A.  contact prints

    B.  enlargements

    C.  montages

    D.  murals

**Rationale A**

**Competency 12**
**Knowledge of the processes of film**

**Skill 12.1**
**Identify and demonstrate knowledge of materials, tools, processes used to create films.**

**Question 12.1**
**Of major importance to a stage-set design is it's**

    A.  fidelity to detail

    B.  ease of scenery shifting

    C.  effectiveness in interpreting a script

    D.  imaginative combinations of stock units

**Rationale C**

**Skill 12.2**
**Demonstrate an understanding of the organization of visual elements and the selection of media for expressive effect.**

**Question 12.2**
**Of the following, the LATEST trend in modern stage production is the**

      A.  theatre in the round

      B.  proscenium arch stage

      C.  apron stage

      D.  revolving stage

**Rationale  A**

**Skill 12.3**
**Identify techniques and methods appropriate for k-12 <u>film</u> instruction.**

**Question 12.3**
**The most powerful factor in a stage design is**

      A.  texture

      B.  form

      C.  color

      D.  line

**Rationale  D**

## Competency 13
## Knowledge of the processes of video

**Skill 13.1**
**Identify and demonstrate knowledge of the technologies, materials, and equipment necessary for creating video art.**

**Question 13.1**
**Ten dollar throw away cameras are still popular but increasingly the cost of developing pictures is further reduced by using a:**

    A. video streaming

    B. scanner

    C. drug store self developing machine

    D. digital camera

**Rationale  D**

**Skill 13.2**
**Demonstrate an understanding of the organization of visual elements and the selection of media for expressive effect.**

**Question 13.2**
**Scrap book collections are putting those vast collections of home pictures into a mixed media home museum.  One page may have used:**

    A. stencils, watercolors,

    B. wood block printing, pen and ink

    C. feathered paper, matting techniques

    D. All the above (and endless more combinations)

**Rationale  D**

**Skill 13.3**
**Identify techniques and methods appropriate for k-12 instruction.**

**Question 13.3**
**Halloween costumes offer wonderful opportunity for mixed media creativity. The human face could be the canvas for mixed media because:**

     A. hair is spray painted wild sparkles

     B. noses of clowns use red rubber balls

     C. antennas can be made from pipe cleaners

     D. balloon hats can be adorned

**Rationale  B**
**It is the only answer that relates to the face. The other adornments are to the head. ( It's a trick question because a lot of words bring your mind in the wrong direction such as costume. You must stay glued to the actual question asked.)**

**Competency 14**
**Knowledge of computer applications.**

**Skill 14.1**
**Identify and demonstrate knowledge of computer technology for computer generated imagery.**

**Question 14.1**
**A computer file name extension that signifies that a file is a picture is**

     A. .com

     B. .txt

     C. .org

     D. .bmp

**Rationale D**

**Skill 14.2**
**Demonstrate an understanding of the organization of visual elements and the selection of media for expressive effect.**

**Question 14.2**
**What is a technique used by computer software programs that change the width and length of a photograph**

A. crop marks

B. crosshatch

C. deckle edge

D. copy fitting

**Rationale A**

**Skill 14.3**
**Identify techniques and methods appropriate for k-12 instruction.**

**Question 14.3**
**A beginning class in computer applications for art would include**

A. drawing circles freehand

B. cut and paste of clip art

C. modification of cartoon strips text

D. fine art reproduction

**Rationale B**

Competency 15 Knowledge of concept art

**Skill 15.1**
Identify and demonstrate knowledge of the processes and distinctly personal ways the artist handles the production of conceptual art.

**Question 15.1**
Monet works as an impressionist painting include

     A. Sunrise: An impression

     B. Old St. Lazare station

     C. The Terrace at Ste. adresse

     D. Les Nympheas

**Rationale C**

**Skill 15.2**
Identify techniques and methods of <u>conceptual art</u> appropriate for k-12 instruction.

**Question 15.2**
A pop artist often use commercial art subjects and techniques in their statements about the contemporary scene. One known for his BRILO BOXES is

     A. Andy Warhol

     B. George Segal

     C. Jim Dine

     D. Clas Oldenburg

**Rationale A**

## Competency 16
**Knowledge of media: materials, hazards, and maintenance  4%**

**Skill 16.1**
**Identify hazardous materials that are commonly used in art procedures.**

**Question 16.1**
**It is unwise to keep items such as _____ in small containers.**

      A.  felt tip markers with obnoxious odors

      B.  pastels (dust)

      C.  irons in the classroom (used to straighten paper)

      D.  Turpentine

**Rationale  D**

**Skill 16.2**
**Recognize procedures required for proper maintenance of basic tools used in drawing, painting, sculpture, printmaking, ceramics, fibers, metals, mixed media.**

**Questions for 16.2 a**
**To maintain paint brushes never**

       A. stand a brush on the bristles

       B. rinse it in solvent

       C. protect your brushes from moths

       D. use plain soap to clean brushes

**Rationale A**

**Question 16.2 b**
**After planishing a silver surface for decoration the work should be**

       A. polished heavily on a buffing wheel

       B. cleaned with emery cloth

       C. cleaned with coarse steel wool

       D. polished as little as possible

**Rationale D**

**Question 16.2 c**
**A two handled egg-shaped jar used for general storage purposes is known as**

       A. apse

       B. abacus

       C. scale

       D. amphora

**Rationale  D**

**Question 16.2 d**
To prevent shattering due to thermal shock, the kiln door should never be opened until the pyrometer registers no more than

    A. 1000 F degrees

    B. 200 F degrees

    C. 500 F degrees

    D. 350 F degrees

**Rationale B**

**Competency 17**
**Knowledge of the source for forming ideas.**

**Skill 17.1**
**Recognize natural environments and constructed environments as starting points for making art.**

**Question 17.1**
Handsome materials, a great stone wall cypress wood and large expanses of glass characterize the living room of TALIESIN, the Wisconsin home of

    A. Philip Webb

    B. Frank Lloyd Wright

    C. Marcel Breuer

    D. Edward Morse

**Rationale B**

**Skill 17.2**
**Recognize inner feelings and imagination as starting points for making art.**

**Question 17.2**
**Highly realistic rendering of the subconscious mind is a good description of the paintings of**

    A. Kandinsky

    B. Dali

    C. Miro

    D. Pollock

**Rationale  B**

**Skill 17.3**
**Recognize the quests for order and do universal theme as starting points for making art.**

**Question 17.3**
**Influences of the hard, sharp precision of a machine age are MOST evident in the paintings of**

     A.  Dufy

     B.  Leger

     C.  Chagall

     D.  Soutine

**Rationale  B**

**Skill 17.4**
**Recognize ordinary experiences as starting points for making art.**

**Question 17.4**
**Grafting Western styles onto tribal themes is MOST evident in the emerging style of the carvings of _____ art.**

     A.  Riparian

     B.  New African

     C.  Chinese

     D.  American Indian

**Rationale  B**

Competency 18
Knowledge of major artists and their works.

Skill 18.1
Identify the scopes and styles of the major schools, movements, and cultural influences of art.

Question 18.1 a
Roman buildings followed the Greek style in

      A.  architectural details and use of the portico

      B.  stressing the importance of the interior

      C.  the use of circular form

      D.  the extensive use of marble

RATIONALE A

Question 18.1 b
The aim of the Romantic Movement was

      A.  spontaneity

      B.  moderation

      C.  intellectualization

      D.  introspection

RATIONALE A

**Question 18.1 c**
**Impressionism was interested in**

      A. fleeting aspects of nature

      B. formal organization

      C. dynamic materialism

      D. spatial vitality

**RATIONALE A**

**Skill 18.2**
**Arrange art developments or movements in chronological order.**

**Question 18.2 a**
**Early Christian art in Europe reflected all the following EXCEPT**

      A. Hellenistic traditional representation

      B. figure drawing from nature

      C. intricate combinations of the Celts

      D. decorative patterns from the East

**RATIONALE B**

**Question 18.2 b**
**Of the following, the names which are NOT grouped in chronological order are:**

      A. Giotto, Van Eyck, Botticelli, Veronese

      B. Poussin, Boucher, David, Delacroix

      C. Pissaro, Millet, Cezanne, Courbet

      D. Michelangelo, Houdon, Rodin, Lurent

**RATIONALE C**

**Question 18.2 c**
**Painting in the late 19th century showed Eastern influence in all of the following EXCEPT**

    A.  clear, pure color

    B.  flat pattern effects

    C.  finesse of line and contour

    D.  atmospheric effects

**RATIONALE D**

**Skill 18.3**
**Identify visual characteristics in works of art that represent a noteworthy departure from other works in a given period.**

**Question 18.3 a**
**Of the following, the FIRST statues ever to show smiles were those of the**

    A.  Romans

    B.  Persians

    C.  Hellenistic Cretans

    D.  archaic Greeks

**RATIONALE D**

**Question 18.3 b**
**The visionary and mystic painter among the late 19th century American painters was**

    A. Eakins

    B. Homer

    C. Ryder

    D. Sargent

**RATIONALE C**

**Question 18.3 c**
**The Cubist movement**

    A. was brief with little influence

    B. has had endless consequences in art

    C. was limited to Braque and Picasso

    D. was a return to academic principles

**RATIONALE B**

**Skill 18.4**
**Identify relationships between specific artists and works of art.**

**Question 18.4 a**
**Aside from painting, Rembrandt was also renowned for his _____**

    A. sculpture

    B. prints

    C. frescoes

    D. architectural designs

**RATIONALE B**

**Question 18.4 b**
**Michelangelo's ADAM AND EVE fresco in the Sistine Chapel**

    A. has sweeping movements which foretell the Baroque

    B. stresses quiet simplicity and ethereal mood

    C. over-dramatizes the figures

    D. represents the figures in real space

**RATIONALE A**

**Question 18.4 c**
**Glass sculpture is made by this famous artist**

    A. Cartier

    B. Steuben

    C. Corning

    D. Faberge

**RATIONALE B**

**Skill 18.5**
**Identify equipment, techniques, and technology used in the production of art forms of specific cultures.**

**Question 18.5 a**
**Japanese temples**

    A. aim at equilibrium between the horizontal and vertical

    B. emphasize the vertical

    C. emphasize the horizontal

    D. emphasize color

**RATIONALE C**

**Question 18.5 b**
**The revolving stage is an innovation which was fully developed in**

    A. France

    B. Germany

    C. Spain

    D. Greece

**RATIONALE B**

**Question 18.5 c**
**In which period of art were stained glass windows introduced for church decoration?**

    A. Roman

    B. Gothic

    C. Renaissance

    D. Futuristic

**RATIONALE B**

**Skill 18.6**
**Compare the relationships between contemporary art and art from the past.**

**Question 18.6 a**
**The MOST important American contribution to the development of architecture has been**
    A.  steel-frame construction

    B.  revolving doors

    C.  elevators

    D.  reinforced concrete

**RATIONALE  A**

**Question 18.6 b**
**FREEDOM OF THE PRESS is associated with the early American printer**

    A.  William Bradford

    B.  Benjamin Franklin

    C.  Stephen Daye

    D.  John Zenger

**RATIONALE  D**

**Question 18.6 c**
**Contemporary sculptors, unlike Bodin, believe that sculpture**
    A.  should express the material of which it is made

    B.  material should be transformed to look like something else

    C.  sculpture should look like living flesh

    D.  should be a detailed imitation of painting

**RATIONALE  A**

## Competency 19 Knowledge of styles

**Skill 19.1**
Distinguish among styles of art from various cultures and periods.

**Question 19.1**
Contemporary abstract-expressionism has prototypes in the works of

    A.  Klee and Kandinsky

    B.  Schmidt-Rutloff and Pechstein

    C.  Kokoschka and Soutine

    D.  Rohlfs and Nolde

**RATIONALE  A**

**Skill 19.2**
Identify components in a work of art that characterize a specific style.

**Question 19.2**
Gilt and metal acanthus leaves, laurel wreaths, torches, winged victories, and cornucopias and signatures of the furniture style known as

    A.  Empire

    B.  Victorian

    C.  Jacobean

    D.  Provincial

**RATIONALE   A**

**Skill 19.3**
**Analyze a work of art on the basis of its style**

**Question 19.3**
**The drabber aspects, the loneliness of unpretentious streets the rectangles and the long horizontals of plain facades characterize the paintings of**

      A. Gyorgy Kepes

      B. Edward Hopper

      C. Morris Graves

      D. George Bellows

**RATIONALE  B**

**Competency 20**
**Analysis of themes, content, and subject matter.**

**Skill 20.1**
**Distinguish among the art terms theme, content, and subject matter.**

**Question 20.1**
**Surrealism had as an aim to**

      A. develop apart from the other arts

      B. express the writing of Freud

      C. figures caught in swirling movement

      D. unification through dynamic movement

**RATIONALE  B**

**Skill 20.2**
**Analyze art works based on specific themes, content, and subject matter.**

**Question 20.2**
**Picasso's mural, GUENICA, emphasizes**

      A. misery and distrust

      B. political corruption

      C. glory and battle

      D. death triumphant

**RATIONALE  D**

<u>Competency</u> **21**
**Recognition of design organization**

**Skill 21.1**
**Describe the visual elements and compositional features in two or more works of art.**

**Question 21.1**
**Both the early Christian and the early Byzantine periods are noted for their**

      A. minarets and fine marble bell towers

      B. enormous stained glass windows

      C. filigree work in metal

      D. mosaic decorations

**RATIONALE   D**

**Skill 21.2**
**Describe the differences or similarities between the visual elements and compositional principles in two or more works of art.**

**Question 21.2**
**Among the following pairs of descriptive words, the pair that may BEST be used to describe a comparison of MOSES by Michelangelo and the Egyptian statue of PHAROAH Ramses II is**

> A. spiral versus frontal
>
> B. open versus closed
>
> C. delicate versus ornate
>
> D. restrained versus unrestrained

**RATIONALE A**

**Skill 21.3**
**Identify works of art that are similar or different in form, style, content, and subject matter.**

**Question 21.3**
In contrast to Florentine painters who were primarily interested in the study of form to express ideas the Venetians strove for

> A. brutal reality
>
> B. abstract conceptions
>
> C. sumptuous magnificence
>
> D. two-dimensional expression

**RATIONALE C**

**Skill 21.4**
**Select from a group of art works those that show the most movement, stability simplicity, or complexity**

**Question 21.4 a**
**The adjectives *delicately proportioned sense of balance and calm* apply to _____ architecture.**

    A. Greek

    B. Medieval

    C. Hellenistic

    D. Roman

**RATIONALE A**

<u>**Competency 22**</u>
**Recognition of the organization of the artistic process.**

**Skill 22.1**
**Describe the media and processes used in works of art.**

**Question 22.1**
**Mountains in a water color can MOST effectively be made to appear farther away by**

    A. green against a red background

    B. yellow against a blue background

    C. orange against a blue background

    D. black against a yellow background

**RATIONALE B**

**Skill 22.2**
**Identify the objects themes, events, and symbols in selected works of art.**

**Question 22.2**
The best source of visual material to enrich a classroom lesson on the principles of still life composition may be found in the works of:

    A.  Signac

    B.  Chagall

    C.  Cezanne

    D.  Utrillo

**RATIONALE   C**

**Skill 22.3**
**State the main ideas presented in selected works of art.**

**Question 22.3**
**The main idea of Mayan art was**

    A.  the human form

    B.  tigers

    C.  death faces

    D.  the serpent - bird

**RATIONALE   D**

**Skill 22.4**
**Describe the differences in expressive effects among works of art**

**Question 22.4**
**Impressionistic color and that which was of value in the whole Renaissance tradition were combined in the paintings of**

    A. Cezanne

    B. Henri Rousseau

    C. Toulouse Lautrec

    D. Monet

**RATIONALE A**

**Skill 22.5**
**Describe how visual qualities combine to give a work of art a particular expressive form.**

**Question 22.5**
**Egyptian mural paintings show**

    A. no feeling for nature

    B. true perspective in depicting garden scenes

    C. subject matter coordinated to a flat surface

    D. realistic colors of human attire

**RATIONALE C**

<u>Competency 23</u>
**Ability to make value judgments**

**Skill 23.1**
**Judge a work of art on how well its visual qualities relate to one another**

**Question 23.1**
**The most important consideration for determining whether a color should be painted on the ceiling of a room is the**

   A. color's affinity to the tone of the floor

   B. color's relationship to the textured or patterned surfaces in the room

   C. effect of space desired

   D. number of openings in the room

**RATIONALE  C**

**Skill 23.2**
**Judge a work of art on how well it creates a vivid and intense emotion or response.**

**Question 23.2**
**His puzzling paintings "The Scream" contain nightmarish and grotesque figures and faces within an atmosphere of wild fantasy.**

   A. Hans Memlins

   B. Hugo Van Der goes

   C. Jan Van Eck

   D. Edward Munch

**RATIONALE  D**

**Skill 23.3**
**Judge a work of art on how well the artist has controlled the medium.**

**Question 23.3**
**When making hand wrought jewelry, the material which is used to imbed rings bracelets, necklaces, etc. while being worked is**

A. gelatin

B. pitch

C. epoxy-cement

D. plaster of Paris

**RATIONALE B**

**Skill 23.4**
**Distinguish between adequate criteria and inadequate criteria**

**Question 23.4**
**A contemporary phase of painting sweeping America, satirizing the** *Cult of the Commonplace,* **is called**

A. abstract expressionism

B. collage

C. pop art

D. art nouveau

**RATIONALE C**

**Skill 23.5**
**Identify non-aesthetic factors that may affect judgment.**

**Question 23.5**
**Evaluation of a work of art should NOT include**

      A.  consideration of subject matter

      B.  cost

      C.  materials used

      D.  style

**RATIONALE   B**

**Competency 24**
**Knowledge of philosophies and theories**

**Skill 24.1**
**Identify major aesthetic philosophies and theories**

**Question 24.1**
**Individual styles which have established costume trends include all of the following EXCEPT**

      A.  extravagant elaborate hats – Hedda Hopper

      B.  forward tilted hat with feathers – Empress Eugenie

      C.  beanie – Duchess of Windsor

      D.  pillbox hat worn far back – Jacqueine Kennedy

**RATIONALE   A**

## Competency 25
**Knowledge of cultural influence and perspectives**

**Skill 25.1**
Identify cultural influences and perspectives that shape particular aesthetic theory or practice.

**Question 25.1**
Peasants singing, working, dancing, and feasting, are shown vividly in the paintings of:

    A.  Velasquez

    B.  Goya

    C.  El Greco

    D.  Murillo

**RATIONALE   D**

## Competency 26
**Ability to apply theories**

**Skill 26.1**
Demonstrate knowledge of cultural perspective as it affects perception and artistic experience.

**Question 26.1**
Early Christian sculpture is characterized by:

    A.  large cult statues

    B.  life size representations of human figures

    C.  sculptural reliefs with special depth

    D.  small-scale forms and surface decoration

**RATIONALE   D**

## Competency 27
**Knowledge of the theoretical bases of curriculum and instruction.**

### Skill 27.1
**Recognize how social and psychological foundations of art education define implications for art learning.**

**Question 27.1**
**To understand a pupils readiness for advanced work**

    A. ask a parent how long the pupil takes to do math homework

    B. observe the pupil as he works on practice material in class

    C. Pose questions to cooperative learning groups to ascertain answers as to how they arrived at an answer

    D. use test scores

**RATIONALE B**

### Skill 27.2
**Identify events, persons, and <u>philosophies</u> instrumental in the historical development of art education**

**Question 27.2**
**Of the following, the main reasons why psychologists warn against over-emphasis of the rewards and punishment motivation:**

    A. it ignores the more effective stimulus of inner satisfaction

    B. it inevitably leads to a listless class atmosphere

    C. it has little or no influence with the bright child

    D. it often leads by easy stages to corporal punishment

**RATIONALE A**

## Competency 28
Knowledge of the practical bases of curriculum and instruction.

### Skill 28.1
Identify long-range and short-range goals for an art program.

**Question 28.1**
Once a class is hopelessly behind the time schedule for the curriculum what should the teacher do at midyear?

    A.  Reduce the content to the most vital topics with the aid of the Chairman

    B.  Speed up your teaching, double assignments, omit visual aids, reduce the number of tests

    C.  Develop mimeographed notes for study at home, test pupils

    D.  Proceed at the pace, inform chairman, explain that these pupils are getting excellent training on fewer topics and will fare better even though you will not be able to go through all objectives.

**RATIONALE  A**


### Skill 28.2
Identify components of curriculum development, including long-range and short-range goals, student performance objectives sequential instructional units, <u>teaching strategies</u>, and assessment techniques.

**Question 28.2**
Which of the following is generally a sound principle of questioning for the teacher to follow?

    A.  the pupil must feel a need or desire to find a solution

    B.  the problem situation must come from the experiences of the pupil

    C.  there should not be a barrier between the pupil and the solution

    D.  the problem should be clear cut and be solvable in only one way

**RATIONALE  C**

**Skill 28.3**
**Identify student needs and abilities, including those of special populations such as handicapped, bilingual, limited English and gifted and talented students.**

**Question 28.3**
**A gifted student asks a question that the art teacher cannot immediately answer. The best way for a teacher to handle the situation is to**

 A.  attempt to answer the question anyway

 B.  admit he does not know and have the answer looked up and reported to the class at the same or next lesson

 C.  state that the question will be answered a future time

 D.  accept the answer of a student who seems to know

**RATIONALE  B**

**Skill 28.4**
**Identify procedures for budget development, including selecting ordering, and inventorying supplies.**

**Question 28.4**
**Which of the following statements best describe zero based budgeting process?**

 A. It examines each item in relation to expected revenues

 B.  It begins with empty accounts to then justify the continuation of the expenditure

 C.  It begins with accounts for the past three years and looks a the history of spending to justify new expenditures

 D.  It integrates long-range planning with the resources provided to meet specific needs

**RATIONALE  B**

**Skill 28.5**
**Identify motivational activities and techniques.**

**Question 28.5**
**Group morale will be higher, as a rule, in classes that are run in which one of the following ways**

    A. Democratic

    B. Autocratic

    C. Laissez-faire

    D. Individual

**RATIONALE A**

**Skill 28.6**
**Identify instructional delivery strategies that are appropriate for student needs and lesson goals and objectives, with consideration for situational constraints.**

**Question 28.6**
**Which one of the following basic suggestions should one carry out first to establish good class management.**

    A. Train the class in distribution of material

    B. Discuss the aims of the year's work

    C. Take out a seating plan

    D. Discuss the required rules for proper class behavior.

**RATIONALE D**

**Skill 28.7**
**Match an aesthetic theory to a classroom practice.**

**Question 28.7**
**The Lemon Test provides a rubric for analyzing educational theory to determine their constitutionality. The constitutional issue that the Lemon Test addresses is**

    A.  free speech

    B.  search and seizure

    C.  establishment of religion

    D.  good and welfare of the students

**RATIONALE  C**
**The Lemon Test was described in Lemon v. Kurtzman and is used to analyze policies and practices in regard to the Establishment Clause of the First Amendment. The test has three parts; if a policy or practice violates any one of the three parts, than the policy or practice violates the establishment clause. The three parts o the lemon test are: 1) Does the policy have a secular purpose? 2) Does the policy advance or inhibit religion? 3) Does the policy allow an entanglement between religion and the school classroom?**

**Skill 28.8**
**Provision for <u>health</u> and safety <u>measures</u>.**

**Question 28.8**
**Children in hospitals that unable to do heavier work can be provided a challenging activity including watercolor because:**

    A.  it can be a pre-writing activity

    B.  spilled paint washes out of linens

    C.  it can increase the dexterity of the hand

    D.  all the above

**RATIONALE  D**

**Skill 28.9**
**Identify techniques for classroom management routines, student-teacher rapport, and <u>student behavior standards</u>.**

**Question 28.9**
Modeling of a behavior by an adult who verbalizes the thinking process, overt self-instruction, and covert self-instruction, are components of:

    A.  rational-emotive therapy

    B.  reality therapy

    C.  cognitive behavior modification

    D.  reciprocal teaching

**RATIONALE C**

**Skill 28.10**
**Demonstrate an understanding of the production use of audio-visual instructional media.**

**Question 28.10**
**Today, the video technologies allow "time-shift" and "place shift" instruction that occurs away from a live teacher. The use of video technology in the classroom could use**

    A.  computer conferencing

    B.  wide area network

    C.  distance education

    D.  all of the above

**RATIONALE D**

**Skill 28.11**
**Identify principles and procedures for evaluating student progress according to objective.**

**Question 28.11**
**What is perhaps the most controversial issue in developmental psychology?**

      A.  interaction and intrapersonal development

      B.  nature v. nurture

      C.  relevance of IQ scores

      D.  change v external events

**RATIONALE  B**

**Skill 28.12**
**Demonstrate an understanding of diagnostic procedures used for identifying entry-level skills of students.**

**Question 28.12**
**Of the following terms, the major aim for giving a standardized test at the beginning of a new course is to:**

      A.  discover weaknesses of previous teaching

      B.  discover interests, attitudes and previously learned material

      C.  give teachers feedback to group classes in terms of ability

      D.  arouse pupil curiosity and provide a base for motivation

**RATIONALE  B**

**Skill 28.13**
**Identify purposes and methods of display.**

**Question 28.13**
**Which statement concerning audio-visual aides is NOT true:**

    A.  may not be used with a page of the textbook

    B.  enables the teacher to observe the class reaction

    C.  may be used with transparencies and with overlays

    D.  they substitute for, rather than supplement instructional techniques

**RATIONALE   D**

**Skill 28.14**
**Identify community resources and their applications to an art program.**

**Question 28.14**
**An appreciation of mural painting may best be heightened by a class:**

    A.  study the reproductions of Rivera

    B.  lectures on the 911 quilt

    C.  visit a local library that may have murals

    D.  homework assignment to find murals in the city

**RATIONALE   A**

**Skill 28.15**
**Identify possible art career choices available to the students.**

**Question 28.15**
**The concept of the starving artist changes dramatically if the career choice is that of:**

A. a high school art teacher

B. restoring old furniture

C. an impressionist painter

D. an architect

**RATIONALE   D**

**Competency 29**
**Knowledge of research, professional organizations, and journals.**

**Skill 29.1**
**Identify concepts in current research.**

**Question 29.1**
Free art for abused children is an organization that:

A. releases anger in abused children through many creative modalities

B. is only available in Arizona

C. has millions of members

D. is limited to one family member per household

**RATIONALE   A**

**Skill 29.2**
**Identify the benefits of membership and participation in professional organizations.**

**Question 29.2**
**ARTtalk.com benefits of membership include all BUT:**

     A. lists art organizations

     B. resource for web links to galleries, magazines workshops

     C. distance learning clinics for masters degree college credit

     D. learn art technique tips

**RATIONALE  C**

**Skill 29.3**
**Identify current professional art journals and art education journals.**

# XAMonline, INC.  21 Orient Ave.  Melrose, MA 02176

Toll Free number 800-509-4128

*TO ORDER Fax 781-662-9268 OR www.XAMonline.com*

## CALIFORNIA SUBJECT EXAMINATIONS   - CSET - 2008

PO#                    Store/School:


Address 1:


Address 2 (Ship to other):

City, State Zip

**Credit card number**_____-_____-_____-_____    expiration_____

**EMAIL** _____

**PHONE**                              **FAX**

| ISBN | TITLE | Qty | Retail | Total |
|------|-------|-----|--------|-------|
| 978-1-58197-595-6 | RICA Reading Instruction Competence Assessment | | | |
| 978-1-58197-596-3 | CBEST CA Basic Educational Skills | | | |
| 978-1-58197-398-3 | CSET French Sample Test 149, 150 | | | |
| 978-1-58197-622-9 | CSET Spanish 145, 146, 147 | | | |
| 978-1-58197-803-2 | CSET MSAT Multiple Subject 101, 102, 103 | | | |
| 978-1-58197-261-0 | CSET English 105, 106, 107 | | | |
| 978-1-58197-608-3 | CSET Foundational-Level Mathematics 110, 111 | | | |
| 978-1-58197-285-6 | CSET Mathematics 110, 111, 112 | | | |
| 978-1-58197-340-2 | CSET Social Science 114, 115 | | | |
| 978-1-58197-342-6 | CSET General Science 118, 119 | | | |
| 978-1-58197-585-7 | CSET Biology-Life Science 120, 124 | | | |
| 978-1-58197-395-2 | CSET Chemistry 121, 125 | | | |
| 978-1-58197-399-0 | CSET Earth and Planetary Science 122, 126 | | | |
| 978-1-58197-224-5 | CSET Physics 123, 127 | | | |
| 978-1-58197-299-3 | CSET Physical Education, 129, 130, 131 | | | |
| 978-1-58197-397-6 | CSET Art Sample Subtest 140 | | | |
| | | | SUBTOTAL | |
| | | | Ship | $8.70 |
| | | | TOTAL | |

www.ingramcontent.com/pod-product-compliance
Lightning Source LLC
Chambersburg PA
CBHW081218170526
45165CB00009B/2865